EXPLORING
BIG BEND

by Barbara A. Donovan illustrated by Stacy Schuett

Harcourt
SCHOOL PUBLISHERS

D1798510

Printed in China

ISBN 10:   0-15-377437-1
ISBN 13:   978-0-15-377437-9

Ordering Options
ISBN 10:   0-15-377149-6 (Grade 5 Collection)
ISBN 13:   978-0-15-377149-1 (Grade 5 Collection)
ISBN 10:   0-15-377898-9 (package of 5)
ISBN 13:   978-0-15-377898-8 (package of 5)

2 3 4 5 6 7 8 9 10   0940   17 16 15 14 13 12 11 10 09

Characters
Cindy, tour guide
Carlos Ortiz
Mr. Ortiz
Mrs. Ortiz
Jack Henry
Emily Henry
Mr. Henry
Mrs. Henry
Chorus

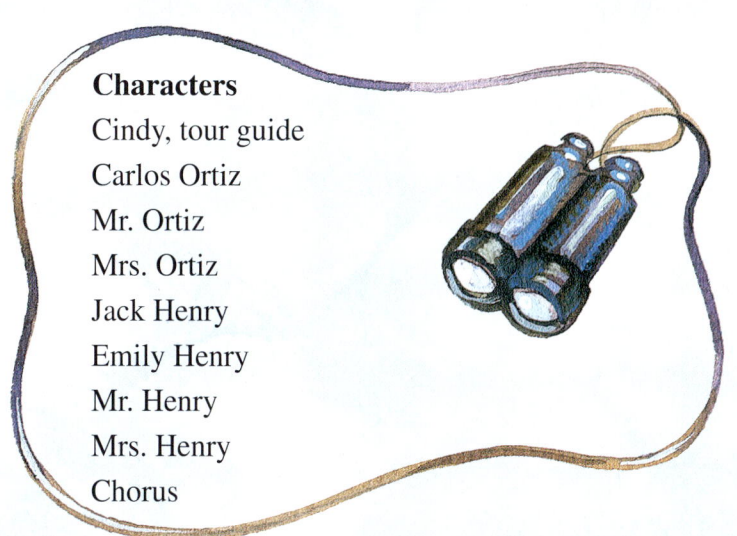

Cindy: Welcome to southern Texas and Big Bend National Park! As is customary, I'll tell you a little bit about the park as we begin the hiking portion of our tour. You will soon see that Big Bend is an exceptional park. At about 800,000 acres, it's one of the largest national parks in the country. We have hundreds of kinds of birds, mammals, and insects living here. Because this is a desert, we also have our share of lizards and snakes. You might see some later in the day. They'll be sunning themselves on rocks to get warm.

3

Carlos: If this is a desert, why isn't it all sand like the ones we see in the movies?

Cindy: You're probably thinking of the Sahara Desert. That's in Africa. All deserts have inadequate rain for most plants and animals, but desert terrain can vary a lot. It might be mostly all sand with very little plant life. Then again, a desert might have the rocky soil with many different kinds of plant life that you see here. The trail we're on is not that grueling. It is, however, a bit rocky, so it's essential that you watch your step. Let's stop for a minute and look around. Tell me what you see.

Mrs. Henry: I see a small spiky plant.

Cindy: That's a lechuguilla. Do you know why it could be called a "soap bush"?

Emily, Jack, and Carlos: I know!

Emily: I said it first!

Jack: No, I said it first!

Mr. Henry: I don't want to hear any bickering. Please give Carlos a chance to answer.

Carlos: It could be called a "soap bush" because long ago Native Americans used to use it to make soap.

Cindy: That's right. They also used to get strong fibers from the stems. They would use the fibers to make mats and ropes and other things they needed. Look at that cactus over there with the flat green pads and the red fruits. That's a prickly pear. The fruits are quite tasty—if you can get them!

Mr. Ortiz: Cindy, what are those marks in the sand over there?

Cindy: Good eyes, Mr. Ortiz! Those are the tracks of a roadrunner. That's one of the birds that is native to this desert. Do you know why it's called a roadrunner?

Emily: Is it because it likes to run along the roads?

Cindy: Yes, it is. This bird doesn't fly very well, so it mostly runs around to get from place to place. If you want to see the tracks of other animals, keep squinting earnestly in sandy spots. You might see lizard tracks or coyote tracks.

Mr. Henry: Are we in any peril from wild animals, Cindy?

Cindy: As long as we mind our own business and do not provoke the animals, we should be safe. Black bears, coyotes, and other animals are wild. Human food is not good for them. If they think you have food, then they're going to try to get it. That's why we keep all the food locked up in special boxes. It's very dangerous to feed the animals. They could get accustomed to looking to humans for their food and not finding it them-selves. That's why it's against the law here to feed them.

Mrs. Ortiz: I'm appalled that people would do something that is potentially so dangerous!

Jack: I've heard about something else that's dangerous here. I've heard that there are scorpions in this desert. Is that true?

Cindy: Yes, but you shouldn't worry about running into one. They come out at night to feed on insects and lizards. If you are camping here, though, you should be careful. Scorpions can climb into your sleeping bags or even your shoes. Always shake things out first before using them.

Mr. Ortiz: Goodness, what's that awful smell?

Cindy: There must be some javelinas around here. They hunt in small packs during the cool morning hours. Oh, look! There they are!

Mr. Ortiz: Are they pigs?

Cindy: Some people think that these animals are equivalent to pigs, but these animals are not even related to them. In fact, the scent gland that makes them smell so terrible is one of the big differences between a pig and a javelina.

Jack: Well, I say, let's keep walking. I want to stay as far away from that smell as I can get.

Cindy: That's fine with me. We're just headed for that stand of cottonwood trees over there. It's starting to get hot, so we'll rest in the shade for a bit. Then we can start our river tour. The truck should already be there with our raft.

Emily: Look up in the sky! Is that a hawk?

Cindy: Actually, that's a peregrine falcon. It's poised to dive for its food. In a dive, these birds can reach speeds of 200 miles (322 km) per hour!

Mr. Henry: Aren't they endangered birds?

Cindy: They are endangered throughout the United States. Lately, they have started coming back in some places, which is quite an achievement. In fact, these regal birds are making nests in the tall buildings in big cities. Here in Texas, this bird is still in danger of becoming extinct. As a result it is still protected here.

Carlos: How far away is the river?

Cindy: It's just on the other side of these trees.

Mrs. Henry: I can't believe how we can go from a desert to the cool shade by the river in just a few yards.

Cindy: This narrow strip of land on either side of the river is an oasis in this desert. Look across the river. That land on the other side is another country. It's Mexico. The river forms the border between our country and Mexico. This river is called the *Rio Grande*.

Mr. Ortiz: Will we be crossing the river into Mexico?

Cindy: No. We'll be traveling down the river, but we'll stay on our side. Your paddle might cross over the line by accident, but we won't land. We need to keep you in the United States.

Mrs. Henry: I love the tranquility of this oasis. I could rest here for hours!

Jack: Do you have mountain lions in the desert?

Cindy: Yes, we have quite a few here in the desert. The mountain lions help keep down the populations of plant-eating animals. If we didn't have mountain lions and coyotes, too, then the number of plants might become insufficient to feed all the animals. We'd end up with only sand, just like the Sahara that Carlos was wondering about.

Emily: That would not be good at all.

Cindy: No, that wouldn't be good. I think we're ready to get into our raft. Check that you buckled your life jackets. We'll be paddling past the steep canyon walls that this river has carved out over thousands of years. Watch for the many birds that fly through this area each spring. Keep your eyes on the shore for more mountain lions or even a black bear. You never know what will decide to come down to the river for a drink.

Chorus: Let's go explore Big Bend by way of the Rio Grande!

Think Critically

1. Tell how pigs and javelinas are alike and different.

2. Summarize the key points of this Readers' Theater.

3. Name one fact and one opinion that Cindy shared with the families. Tell how you decided whether each was a fact or an opinion.

4. Would you like to go on a tour of Big Bend National Park? Explain why or why not.

5. What is the author's main purpose in writing this Readers' Theater? Explain how you know.

 Social Studies

More on Mexico Do research on the Internet or using library resources to learn more about Mexico and its geography. Make a map to summarize your findings.

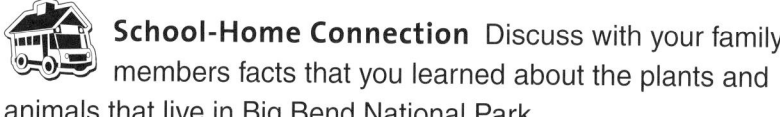 **School-Home Connection** Discuss with your family members facts that you learned about the plants and animals that live in Big Bend National Park.